Everyday Creativity

PROMPTS, ACTIVITIES, AND FAITH-FILLED
PRACTICES TO CULTIVATE YOUR GIFTS

Jena Holliday

Creator of Spoonful of Faith

Ink &
Willow

made
to
create

do not despise small beginnings

Zechariah 4:10, NLT

Contents

Introduction

I've been doodling faces in the margins of notebooks and scribbling words on anything I could get my hands on since I was young. I can't remember a time when I didn't journal. Journaling was a home for my thoughts, dreams, fears, and prayers. As well as everything in between. Around two years ago, after searching far and wide for the perfect journal for a creative spirit like myself, I finally decided I would just make my own. I went to the local craft store, bought a sketchbook, and made a journal.

What I needed was a safe space to store inspiration. A mood board, if you will, that I could open each day to follow the trail of what I placed there last and then keep going. Sometimes I needed it to be a guide— where I could build out creative goals and challenges that would help me move toward the next step. Some days I needed it to help me go deeper into my thoughts, ask the hard questions, and offer my prayers and, at times, tears to God.

I crafted a tool that took my raw ideas and thoughts and organized them in a way that made sense to my creative brain. A journal that pushed me from ideation to execution. And best of all? I built a place that helped me believe God could use all the parts of me, including my creativity, for His glory. And now, I offer this tool to you!

Maybe you've started believing the lie that you aren't creative. Or maybe you feel that what you have to offer isn't enough. Maybe you've always doubted that what God gave you could be used in a way that encourages those around you. Beloved, God gave you gifts, and He wants you to use them! Because your Creator knows that when you take practical steps to honor your creative gift, you glorify Him and shine His light to those around you.

Everyday Creativity will help you nurture your God-given creativity. And not in the hustle-and-grind kind of way that exhausts your soul or seeks accolades. Rather, this tool will encourage you to create from a place that feels free, authentic, faith-led, inspired, and intrinsically motivated.

This journal is a sidekick for your creative journey. You'll walk through a five-part guide that brings your creative ideas to life. If the road gets hard or you feel stuck, no pressure—you have the freedom to put it down (or pick it up) when you need to. When you're ready, there are prompts to help you get out of your head and back to action. There are also blank slates to brain dump, draw, or create whatever you want. On your journey, you'll find space for mood boards, goal setting, creative challenges, and reflection. Take your time making space for new thoughts and ideas to emerge. Ultimately, you'll forge a path through the creative process with resources and challenges to keep you engaged along the way.

Beloved, I hope, like me, you find encouragement and motivation to create within these pages. May you be propelled forward as your God-given creativity blooms and flourishes. And may you discover more of your gifts and use them in confident and joyful worship of the Creator.

Look over the creative map to get a glimpse of where we are headed through the journey of these pages. The prayer after the map will also help put you in the right mindset.

Creative Map

Connecting & Sharing Your Message

Using What You Have

Starting Your Practice

Overcoming Fear & Creative Blocks

Self-Discovery

Start Here

Start over

Dear Lord,

I pray over every heart that uses this journal and desires to use their gifts well. I ask that You empower our hearts with a fire and motivation to create and use our gifts to honor what you've given us. Help us to establish new rhythms and beliefs that keep us consistent in this work and not giving up. Bless the work of our hands and remind us that we do this with You right by our side. I ask that the tools and resources shared throughout this journal be helpful and beneficial to those who take action.

Amen

Self-Discovery

Self-discovery is a powerful part of your creative journey. When you get real about what makes you who you are, then you'll begin to understand how your past has shaped what you make and how you create. In this section, you'll explore more of your history, your personality, your habits, and your ideas and beliefs around creativity. Stay open and honest through the process. I have no doubt you'll learn something interesting about yourself along the way!

All About You

Take a trip down memory lane to honor your creative story. Respond to the questions that follow—go at your own pace. With each answer, reflect on how your unique journey has shaped your creative process, and remember how you fell in love with creating.

How old were you when you first started using your creative gifts?

_____

_____

_____

_____

Share a childhood story where you made or created something.

_____

_____

_____

_____

Who was the first person to encourage your creativity?

_____

_____

_____

_____

What is the best or most memorable thing you have ever created?

_____

_____

_____

_____

_____

_____

What are some of your favorite traits about yourself?

_____

_____

_____

_____

_____

Make a list of things that you feel come easy or natural to you.

_____

_____

_____

_____

_____

For you formed
      my inward parts;
you knitted me together
      in my mother's womb.
I praise you, for I am
      fearfully and
      wonderfully made.

Wonderful are your works;
   my soul knows it very
   well.

Psalm 139:13-14

What are some similarities between how you created as a child and how you create now? What are some differences?

_____

_____

_____

_____

_____

Make a list of what you love about your creative process.

_____

_____

_____

_____

_____

Do you consider yourself persistent, or do you give up easily? Why?

_____

_____

_____

_____

_____

_____

What are some things about yourself you want to work on or change?

_____

_____

_____

_____

_____

_____

_____

_____

_____

List the ways that you think someone you love would describe you.

_____

_____

_____

_____

_____

_____

_____

_____

_____

Going Deeper

Take time to look back over your answers. Does anything stand out or spark further curiosity? Journal your thoughts.

What Is Creativity to You?

Over the years, I have mentored, met, and connected with hundreds of people. I've discovered that everyone has different opinions about creativity. So, at each meeting, I ask, "What is creativity to you?" Below are some of the common replies. What do you think of the different responses?

"I used to think I wasn't creative, but now I'm trying to stop saying that and just create."

"creativity is taking a risk to try something new."

"I honestly haven't felt creative since being a child."

"creativity is very important for me. My great-grandpa gave me a love for drawing and creativity."

"To me it's moving in faith in the assignments God gives us, in the unique way that's individually ours."

Now it's your turn. Fill in the bubbles with what creativity means to you.

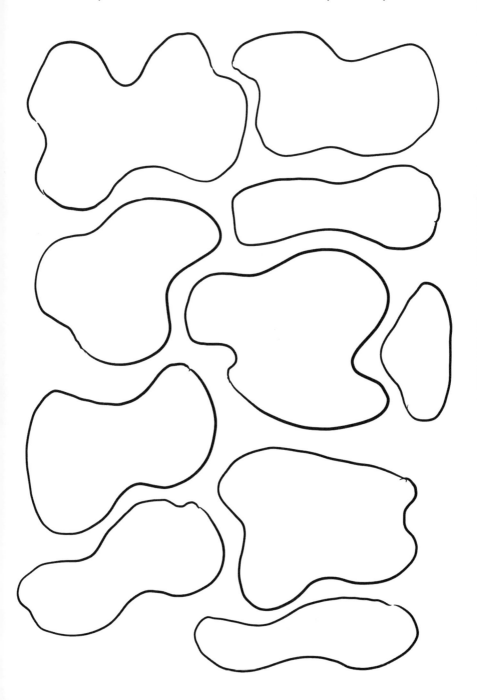

Your Relationship with Creativity

Next, spend time focusing on how you relate to your creative gifts. These questions will help you rediscover what inspires, guides, and rekindles your creative spark. Take your time as you answer each prompt. This can be done in one sitting or at your own pace.

When did you start considering yourself creative? Why?

_____

_____

_____

_____

_____

Can you point to a time when you felt passionate about creating, making, building, or solving something?

_____

_____

_____

_____

_____

Make a list of your favorite creative outlets.

_____

_____

_____

_____

_____

_____

_____

_____

_____

_____

When do you find yourself most filled with ideas and inspiration?

_____

_____

_____

_____

_____

_____

_____

_____

_____

What holds you back from creating?

_____

_____

_____

_____

_____

_____

_____

_____

Share a story of a time when you felt discouraged in your creativity.

_____

_____

_____

_____

_____

_____

_____

_____

_____

When is the last time you used your creative gifts just to create, with no expectations of the outcome?

_____

_____

_____

_____

_____

_____

_____

What are the best words to describe how you feel when you are making something or using your gifts?

_____

_____

_____

_____

_____

_____

_____

_____

On a perfect day with no constraints, what is one thing you would like to do, see, create, or experience?

_____

_____

_____

_____

_____

Do you have any hopes for your creative talents or gifts? If so, what are they?

_____

_____

_____

_____

_____

List five words you want to use to describe yourself but haven't had the courage to use yet.

_____

_____

_____

_____

_____

Your Creative Personality Type

Knowing your personality—and how it connects with your creativity—is an important piece to understanding the way you work and create. By understanding your creative personality, you gain insight into how you approach the creative process, which helps you lean on your strengths, know your weaknesses, and navigate challenges more effectively.

The personalities compiled below are a mash-up from various research and quizzes. These are some of the most popular types of creative personalities.

Take a moment to check the boxes next to ones you feel represent you. This isn't definitive but will give you a good idea of some of your strengths and blind spots. Knowing these will help you understand how you work best, providing a more harmonious creative journey.

ROMANTIC

- ☐ Enjoys thinking through ideas and visions
- ☐ Introspective
- ☐ Uses their creativity to evoke new perspectives
- ☐ Passion-driven
- ☐ Seeks inspiration in all things

A Romantic Creative: *Madeleine L'Engle, writer*

INTELLECT

- ☐ Curious for truth
- ☐ Looks for bigger picture
- ☐ Interested in learning new things
- ☐ Deep thinker
- ☐ Intellectual

An Intellect Creative: *Elizabeth Catlett, sculptor and graphic artist*

OPTIMIST

- ☐ Big imagination
- ☐ Looks for hidden meaning
- ☐ Empathetic
- ☐ Hopeful
- ☐ Leads intuitively

An Optimist Creative: *Georgia O' Keeffe, painter*

ARCHITECT

- ☐ Problem solver
- ☐ Committed to mastering their craft
- ☐ Energetic
- ☐ Self-sufficient
- ☐ Natural leadership qualities

Architect Creatives: *Maya Angelou and Toni Morrison, writers and activists*

EXPLORER

- ☐ Stays curious
- ☐ Storyteller
- ☐ Enthusiastic and takes initiative
- ☐ Likes to experiment and try new things
- ☐ Open to taking risks

An Explorer Creative: *Julia Child, chef*

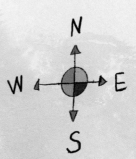

Reflect and Celebrate

Self-discovery and awareness are an ongoing journey, and you won't figure it all out through this journal. Let this be a launching point by taking every piece of what you've gathered here to help you understand even more of the beautiful being God created you to be. Be open to making improvements in areas you desire to change, but also be kind to yourself as you work through them. Don't be afraid of what you uncover, but let it help you connect more with what you make and create.

Use the space below to reflect on your personal self-discoveries.

_____

_____

_____

_____

_____

_____

_____

_____

_____

_____

_____

_____

_____

And don't forget to celebrate each part of the journey!

One way you can celebrate today? Curate a celebratory playlist of songs that uplift and inspire you. Dance or sing along as a way to honor your completion of this section.

Be Encouraged

There are so many incredible artists out there. If you ever need to be inspired by fellow creatives, take time to read through these quotes.

The artist begins with a vision—a creative operation requiring an effort. Creativity takes courage.

—HENRI MATISSE

I admire women who are open and vulnerable about the self-doubt that happens in the creative process and yet go forward and do it anyway.

—AARTI SEQUEIRA

Overcoming Fear & Creative Blocks

Have you ever doubted your creativity? Maybe someone's offhand remark or response caused you to stop using your gifts or doubt yourself. Maybe you feel like you are hiding your creative potential, unsure whether what you have is enough. Or perhaps you feel paralyzed when it comes to facing new challenges, trying new things, or exploring new ideas. When doubt creeps in, we feel like what we are making is "bad work." Being afraid can be one of our greatest hurdles in using our creative gifts.

In this section, we will explore your biggest dreams and ideas and tackle your inner critic to break free from your limiting beliefs. We'll learn new creative activities that will encourage and affirm your God-given gifts. It's time to rise above our fears and be the creatives we were meant to be.

What's Holding You Back?

Nearly all of us have faced fear and insecurity in our creative journeys: What if it doesn't work like I imagined? What if I'm not skilled enough? What if my best isn't accepted?

In the rocks below, identify and label the obstacles that are holding you back right now.

Let's walk through some tough questions to discover what might be standing in the way of your creative endeavors.

What does being a successful creative look like to you?

_____

_____

_____

_____

_____

Share a time you compared yourself and your gifts to someone else and theirs.

_____

_____

_____

_____

_____

What is the biggest failure you've ever faced, and what have you learned from it?

_____

_____

_____

_____

List things from your past or present that feel like blocks to your creativity, such as self-doubt, lack of inspiration, or time constraints.

_____

_____

_____

_____

What de-motivates you or pushes you further away from your goals?

_____

_____

_____

_____

_____

_____

Make a list of creative activities you have given up on.

_____

_____

_____

_____

_____

List three things you fear you'll get wrong when starting a project.

_____

_____

_____

_____

_____

What, if any, recurring thoughts or self-doubts tend to hinder your creative process?

_____

_____

_____

_____

_____

_____

_____

_____

List the ways in which you procrastinate.

_____

_____

_____

_____

_____

_____

_____

_____

_____

You have the courage to begin again.

What Is True?

When I was developing my creative practices, I remember being hit with a lot of feelings of comparison. Negative thoughts would swirl in my head, and it felt difficult to change my perspective. In my quiet time, I remember praying about my problem and thinking about the words of Romans 10:17: "Faith comes from hearing, and hearing through the word of Christ." My heart knew I needed to hear something good and true to get out of my own head.

But what was true? I grabbed a sheet of paper and divided it into two columns. One was labeled Truth, and the other was labeled Lie. I started with all the negative thoughts that were holding me back and added those to the lie column. Then I spent time adding to the truth side, using scriptures, affirmations, quotes, or words I personally received from loved ones or from the Lord.

While things didn't magically change overnight, the story I told myself impacted my mood, my beliefs, and my motivation. I might not be able to completely avoid feeling self-doubt or comparison, but when I have that foundation of what is true, I can confidently show up anyway as those feelings creep in. I don't have to run from my feelings, because I have a powerful tool to face them head-on. This practice has totally transformed my faith and boosted my confidence.

As the truth of God's Word pierces through the lies and strengthens your heart, may you be encouraged in your creativity and trust in the gifts you hold. May you tap into your faith to believe, even in the darkest of moments, that He works all things together for good.

Truth and Lies Activity

On the following pages are two columns labeled *Truth* and *Lies*. On the truth side, write down words and affirming statements you have received from others, scriptures the Lord has highlighted to you, and things you know to be true. On the lies side, write down thoughts you struggle with that are untrue or that are holding you back.

When finished, take time to read the Truth column aloud to yourself so you can hear the truths and God's Word. This practice can be a source of encouragement and peace in your life.

Need a little help getting started? Following this exercise is a small resource of scriptures with words to pull from to build out your list.

TRUTH

LIES

TRUTH	LIES
_____	_____
_____	_____
_____	_____
_____	_____
_____	_____
_____	_____
_____	_____
_____	_____
_____	_____
_____	_____
_____	_____
_____	_____
_____	_____
_____	_____
_____	_____
_____	_____
_____	_____

Speak Good Things

On this page, you'll find scriptures with words to pull from to build out your Truth and Lies Activity list on the previous spread.

You are creative and made in the image of a creative God:

EPHESIANS 2:10
PSALM 139:14
EXODUS 35:35
PSALM 104:24
ROMANS 12:6
1 TIMOTHY 4:14
2 CORINTHIANS 5:17
ROMANS 1:20

JEREMIAH 10:12
GENESIS 1:27
PROVERBS 22:29
EXODUS 35:31-32
EXODUS 31:1-6

You are not a failure:

PHILIPPIANS 4:13
PROVERBS 3:5-6
JEREMIAH 29:11
JAMES 1:2-4
ISAIAH 41:10
2 CORINTHIANS 4:16
PHILIPPIANS 1:6
2 CORINTHIANS 12:9-10
LAMENTATIONS 3:22-23

You can trust God
for your future:

PSALM 23:4
PSALM 27:1
PSALM 46:1-3
JOHN 14:27
DEUTERONOMY 31:6
ISAIAH 41:13
DEUTERONOMY 3:22
LUKE 12:7

You are loved and
accepted:

PSALM 139:13-14
EPHESIANS 1:4
ROMANS 10:11-13
ROMANS 15:7
ACTS 10:34-35
GALATIANS 3:28
EPHESIANS 3:17-19
ROMANS 8:35, 38-39

You can overcome
rejection:

PSALM 94:14
JOHN 15:18
PSALM 27:10
ROMANS 8:31
ISAIAH 49:1

Note to Self

As you work on developing more positive thoughts, it's important to also watch how you speak to yourself. This page is filled with hopeful affirmations and encouraging words you can use as you build your arsenal of affirming truths. Take a moment to read them out loud to yourself. Then, on the next page, practice creating a few of your own.

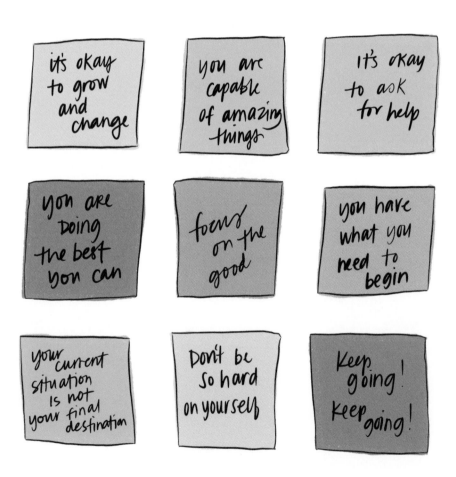

My Creative
Affirmation Statement

Choose one of the affirmations from the "Note to Self" section, or create a new one that affirms you and your unique creative gifts. Think of something that you can read to yourself often that will encourage you right now in your journey.

　　Use the space below to write, letter, or sketch it out.

What Pushes
You Forward?

Let's dig deeper into what empowers you and pushes you toward moving
past fear and having freedom to create. As you answer these questions,
I hope you'll discover your sources of inspiration and strengths to motivate
you in your creative process. Allow yourself some time to sit and respond
thoughtfully.

*Take a moment to recall the last time you felt proud of yourself.
What happened?*

_____

_____

_____

_____

_____

What are some of your biggest dreams, goals, or desires?

_____

_____

_____

_____

_____

What are three goals you would like to achieve within the next three months?

_____

_____

_____

_____

_____

List three mentors in your creative field whom you can learn from.

_____

_____

_____

_____

_____

What inspires you?

_____

_____

_____

_____

_____

_____

What are some things you have always wanted to try?

_____

_____

_____

_____

_____

If you could choose one thing from that list to try this week, what would it be?

_____

_____

_____

_____

_____

Make a list of people you know who never give up.

_____

_____

_____

_____

_____

_____

Stand firm in your faith, be courageous, be strong.

1 corinthians 16:13, RSV

Share about a time when you were resilient.

_____

_____

_____

_____

_____

List what might happen if people reject your creative work.

_____

_____

_____

_____

_____

Now, list what might happen if people accept your creative work.

_____

_____

_____

_____

_____

_____

Make a list of people who have encouraged you in your creative gifts.

_____

_____

_____

_____

_____

_____

_____

List the things you are ready to rid yourself of—things in your home, in your closet, and in your heart. Imagining areas to declutter empowers you to take steps toward a clearer, more positive space and mindset.

_____

_____

_____

_____

_____

_____

_____

_____

_____

Draw the things that bring you the most joy.

Finding Your Creative Why

Look at your responses on the last few pages. Take a moment to use the following worksheet to get more clarity behind why you create. Often, connecting to your heart can motivate you to push past obstacles.

Develop a why statement. As you continue to ask yourself why to each response you give below, you will get closer to a more heart-level understanding of what is driving you forward. Use as many or as few whys as necessary to get to your clearest statement. Don't worry if it's not perfect; you can always come back and change it.

Here's an example:

I create because . . .
> I ENJOY MAKING ART AND SHARING IT WITH OTHERS.

Why?
> I BELIEVE ART IS SOMETHING THAT CAN HEAL PEOPLE.

Why?
> WHEN I USE MY GIFTS OR SEE OTHERS USING THEIRS, I BELIEVE GOD'S LOVE WORKS THROUGH IT.

> I CREATE BECAUSE I ENJOY SHARING CREATIVITY AND I BELIEVE ART HEALS AND GOD'S LOVE WORKS THROUGH IT.

I create because . . .

Why?

Why?

Why?

Why?

I create because . . .

Setting Your Intentions and Goals

Let's start to set some creative intentions for how you'd like to push yourself more creatively in this season.

What are some of the ways you'd like to challenge yourself creatively? What creative goals or ambitions do you have? Maybe it's as simple as committing to keeping a journal or planning time to do an activity each month. Take some time to write out three ideas, small to large, that you can start working toward. Then, in the lined space beside each of your goals, list up to three first steps you can take to get started on that goal.

Here's an example:

SMALL GOAL:
I WANT TO
PLAN TO KEEP
A JOURNAL.

STEP 1: GO TO A STORE AND PICK OUT A JOURNAL.

STEP 2: MAP OUT IN MY CALENDAR THE DAYS I WILL JOURNAL.

STEP 3: SET MY ALARM FOR EACH DAY I AM PLANNING TO WRITE.

SMALL GOAL:

_____
_____
_____
_____
_____
_____
_____
_____

MEDIUM GOAL:

_____
_____
_____
_____
_____
_____
_____
_____

LARGE GOAL:

_____
_____
_____
_____
_____
_____
_____
_____

Creating a Plan for Progress

Now, let's take it one step further. Break each of your goals or intentions into smaller, achievable, and actionable steps. By doing this activity, you are creating a plan to progress in your goals.

For example, if your goal is to create a new recipe, you might break it down into setting a schedule to work on the recipe, creating a mood board of ideas, and making your new recipe.

Your action steps might be to map out two days each week this month to try the recipe, go on Pinterest to get mood board ideas and gather a list of ingredients, experiment in the kitchen on the scheduled days, and take notes during cooking time.

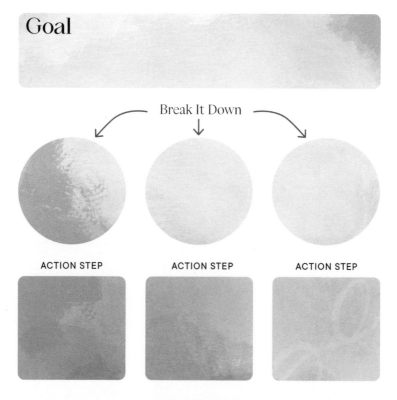

Goal

Break It Down

ACTION STEP

ACTION STEP

ACTION STEP

Reflect and Celebrate

Overcoming obstacles and finding courage to progress in creating can take time. But doing the work to weed out the negative thoughts and lies while holding on to truth will propel you forward. Speak good things to yourself, beloved. Ask God to help you find the right words to affirm what He's already placed in you. Trust that as you take small steps forward, you will gain momentum to propel you toward the goals you have set.

Use the space below for your personal reflections on this section.

_____

_____

_____

_____

_____

_____

_____

_____

_____

_____

Don't forget to celebrate!

Make your favorite coffee or tea, curl up in your favorite cozy spot, and savor the moment. Appreciate the effort you've put into this chapter and the work you've completed so far.

Be Encouraged

There are so many incredible artists out there. If you ever need to be inspired by fellow creatives, take time to read through these quotes.

A self-respecting artist must not fold his hands on the pretext that he is not in the mood.

—PYOTR ILYICH TCHAIKOVSKY

I define creativity
as taking something
and _making_ it into
something else. Yes, this is
demonstrated by artists,
engineers, and chefs, but
it's also done by problem-
solvers, thinkers, listeners,
and helpers. The world
needs people who will use
what they have to build
something better.

—DANIELLE COKE BALFOUR

Starting Your Practice

Consistency is one of the best ways to build your creative practice. This can be through sketching, journaling, setting aside weekly creative dates, and being attentive to how you tap into your creativity on an ongoing basis. The more you show up, the more you get a chance to gain experience, perfect your craft, and become more disciplined in using your gifts. In this section, we will dive into assessing your current practice, discovering your hopes for what's next, and giving you practical steps and tools to cultivate a consistent creative practice.

Showing Up

Take a moment to be honest about your relationship with showing up consistently as you work through the questions below. This can be done in one sitting or at your own pace.

When you've kept a sketchbook, journal, or ideas book, what did you fill it up with?

_____

_____

_____

_____

_____

How do you keep track of inspiration?

_____

_____

_____

_____

_____

_____

How often do you engage in creative activities?

_____

_____

_____

_____

_____

_____

_____

_____

When was the last time you felt like you were disciplined and consistent in something?

_____

_____

_____

_____

_____

_____

_____

Make a list of things you wish you were more consistent in.

_____

_____

_____

_____

_____

_____

_____

_____

Make a list of things you are good at showing up and being consistent for.

_____

_____

_____

_____

_____

_____

_____

Visualize Your Perfect Creative Day

Visualize your perfect day. In the space below, you can use words, drawings, symbols, or anything else you feel will be helpful for capturing what you just visualized. Feeling stuck? Use the questions at the bottom of the page to help prompt some ideas.

Where would you find yourself?

Are you indoors or outside? Is it cozy or a bit chaotic? What does the environment look, smell, and feel like? How is your mood? What do you eat and drink? Are you making or experiencing something new? If so, what are you making? What materials are you using?

Your Typical Day

What is your current daily routine? Lay out what a day in your life looks like by creating a road map. Have fun with it! Include symbols, signs, road delays, and more.

Your Typical Day

Take it further by mapping out your typical day in calendar format this time.

Daily

DATE _____

SCHEDULE

7:00 AM

8:00 AM

9:00 AM

10:00 AM

11:00 AM

12:00 PM

1:00 PM

2:00 PM

3:00 PM

4:00 PM

5:00 PM

6:00 PM

7:00 PM

8:00 PM

9:00 PM

10:00 PM

11:00 PM

TO DO

_____

_____

_____

_____

NOTES

_____

_____

_____

_____

_____

Making Space

As you look at your average day, what open time do you have? What things can be shifted, if needed, to make more time to dedicate to your creative projects?

Worshipful Creativity

When was the last time you used your creative gifts solely to honor God? Making something or creating just because we have been gifted the ability to do so can feel difficult!

What has helped me more times than I can count is doing it as an act of worship to God. Creating as worship to my Creator revives me and allows me to clear my mind and remove the pressure of making something. I've also found that some of my most touching works of art and memorable creative projects have been birthed from that space of simply creating to honor the gift and the Giver.

Allow yourself time to dwell on your relationship with creativity as an act of worship. At your own pace, read and answer the questions below.

Share a time when you felt deeply connected to God.

_____

_____

_____

_____

What does worship look like to you?

_____

_____

_____

_____

Describe the most meaningful thing you ever made or created. How long did it take you? How did it make you or others feel? What was the process like to make it?

_____

_____

_____

_____

_____

_____

_____

What do you think about using creativity as worship?

_____

_____

_____

_____

_____

_____

_____

_____

_____

Your Creative Space

Environment plays a huge role in how we are inspired and motivated to create, pursue our passions, and work. Your space should help you feel safe to create. Take your time answering each prompt as you consider your environment.

What does your creative space look like?

_____

_____

_____

_____

_____

_____

_____

What do you enjoy about the process of creating?

_____

_____

_____

_____

_____

_____

List things that make you feel safe.

_____

_____

_____

_____

_____

_____

_____

_____

List things that make you feel loved.

_____

_____

_____

_____

_____

_____

_____

_____

_____

Keep Track

In the following pages, you'll find space provided for you to start showing up creatively right now. From journal pages to creative session trackers and more, these are meant to help you find a method for gaining consistency in your practice or just learning to track your progress more regularly. Feel free to write, draw, or express whatever comes to mind on each page.

Brain Dumps

Have you ever heard of a brain dump? A brain dump is an exercise where you get to unload all of your unorganized thoughts onto paper. Some experienced artists share that doing this each day helps them get their minds clear and ready to go.

My form of brain dumping is using a journal. Each morning, I write, pray, or dump my thoughts onto the page. It can help with managing my day or just getting my thoughts out. Some days I have no words and just draw instead. It gives me a release and allows me to leave right there on the page anything I can't hold in my head.

Use these pages to freely write, draw, leave your thoughts, or express whatever comes to mind. They can be used for different purposes. For example, on the second page, you might use the brain dump for things you need to get done, listing your top three priorities for the day and three easy things you can do. Breaking your lists and ideas down into smaller, more prioritized lists can help you maintain focus and get things accomplished.

Date [   ] *Brain Dump*

_____   _____
_____   _____
_____   _____
_____   _____
_____   _____
_____   _____
_____   _____
_____   _____
_____   _____
_____   _____
_____   _____

top 3   ### easy 3

_____   _____
_____   _____
_____   _____

Brain Dump

Do it
Past
worship

Creative Sessions Tracker

Devote time to track your dedicated creative sessions. Keeping a record is an important way to stay accountable, measure your growth, and refine your methods. Make sure to note anything you feel that God is showing you during your creative time.

JAN FEB MAR APR MAY JUN JUL AUG SEP OCT NOV DEC
1 2 3 4 5 6 7 8 9 10 11 12 13 14 15 16 17 18 19 20 21 22 23 24 25 26 27 28 29 30 31

Feelings:

grateful for:

on my heart:

notes:

project:

materials:

length of session:

outcomes:

Feelings:

☹ ☹ 😐 🙂 😄

grateful for :

on my heart :

notes :

project :

materials :

length of session :

outcomes :

Feelings:

☹ ☹ 😐 🙂 😄

grateful for:

on my heart:

notes:

project:

materials:

length of session:

outcomes:

Feelings:

☹ ☹ 😐 🙂 😄

grateful for :

on my heart :

notes:

project :

materials:

length of session:

outcomes:

so, *Let us use our gifts.*

Journal Pages

Use these pages to journal your thoughts or any ideas you may have.
No rules! No restrictions!

DATE:

_____

_____

_____

_____

_____

_____

_____

_____

_____

_____

_____

_____

_____

_____

_____

_____

DATE:

DATE:

DATE:

_____

_____

_____

_____

_____

_____

_____

_____

_____

_____

_____

_____

_____

_____

_____

_____

_____

_____

DATE:

DATE:

Monthly Creative Practice

Carve out some time to begin using a monthly creative practice tracker. Even if you can't create every day, keeping track helps you understand your habits, measure progress, and see what you need to work on to create better routines. Allow yourself a moment at the end of the month to reflect on what you learned.

Monthly creative goals:

Skill building
Creating
Planning
Worship + play
Reflecting
Other

Month _____

1	2	3	4	5	6	7
8	9	10	11	12	13	14
15	16	17	18	19	20	21
22	23	24	25	26	27	28
29	30	31

* Color each circle with the color you worked on each day.

Materials I'm using:

Notes & reflections: _____

Fun Prompts for Daily Creativity

While it may feel like creativity sparks at the most random of times, your gifts take practice, and creativity needs to be used often to keep those muscles strong. To guide you in building consistency and also keep it exciting, here are a few prompts you can use to spark creative ideas, open your imagination, and inspire your creative pursuits.

Make a check next to each idea you'd be willing to try for the first time or again. Use your responses from "Your Typical Day" (page 67) to help determine when you can fit a few of these activities in this month.

- ☐ Keep a sketchbook or art journal.
- ☐ Plan an artist date with a fellow creative.
- ☐ Create a travel art-supply kit.
- ☐ Create your own weekly challenge.
- ☐ Take an online class.
- ☐ Dance and move your body.
- ☐ Make a list of the things that get you excited.
- ☐ Get creative with your wardrobe for a week.

- [ ] Grab flowers from the local market or grocery store, and rearrange them for your home.
- [ ] Rearrange a shelf or a room in your home.
- [ ] Cook a new simple recipe.
- [ ] Make a collage or mood board of what inspires you.
- [ ] Fill a page with cursive handwriting.
- [ ] Write out the alphabet in bubble letters.
- [ ] Turn on an audiobook or podcast, and doodle as you listen.
- [ ] Jot down a list of movies, books, and TV shows that make you feel happy.
- [ ] Pick a color. Then go for a walk, and notice all the places you see that one color.

Reflect and Celebrate

As the saying goes, practice makes perfect—or at least makes for progress. Showing up for yourself, even if it is as simple as starting a daily journal or making space for a weekly art date, can really make a world of difference. Let the momentum of the small steps build up to bigger possibilities. You are free to take as much time as you need to learn what works best for helping you use your gifts more consistently.

Use the space below for your personal reflections on this section.

_____

_____

_____

_____

_____

_____

_____

_____

_____

_____

_____

_____

_____

_____

It's celebration time again!

Draw a simple reflection of your emotions and thoughts about ending this section.

Be Encouraged

There are so many incredible artists out there. If you ever need to be inspired by fellow creatives, take time to read through these quotes.

I think what we see in Scripture is that there's so much to be said for the intention of creating. What the intention is and what the process is as we witness the power of creation.

—RUTH CHOU SIMONS

We have to continually be jumping off cliffs and developing our wings on the way down.

—KURT VONNEGUT

Using What You Have

When starting new things, I always look around to see what I already have to use. I'm the middle child of seven, and my siblings and I were a crew of DIYers. Anything that I didn't have at my disposal I'd try to find a way to make, or I'd create a substitute for it. I worked with the leftovers from other activities, tweaking my projects as I went through each phase from beginning to completion. I never allowed limitations of what I didn't have to hold me back. Through this, I learned that everything has a beginner phase and that it's not always going to be perfect. There will be changes and tweaks to every project, so that shouldn't stop us from beginning.

You don't need more to start. Using your abilities with the resources you are holding right now is more important than buying that new, fancy tech product that you don't even know how to work. Being faithful with the little you have to start with will prepare you to be appreciative when you grow to have much more.

In this part, we'll explore various ways of using what you have, being grateful for it, and approaching new things with excitement.

Starting Small

Some of my most sacred and special creations have been birthed in small, intimate beginnings. It's when I am not sure how to start or where things will take me that I begin to discover the childlike nature of the gift of creativity. God rejoices in you showing up at the start.

Take a few moments to answer the questions below. These are designed to help remind you of how some of our most cherished creations unfold from pushing past the uncertainty of small beginnings.

List things you made with little to no materials.

_____

_____

_____

_____

_____

Share a story of a time you didn't feel you had what it took. What happened?

_____

_____

_____

_____

_____

_____

Share a story of a time you overcame despite the odds. What happened?

_____

_____

_____

_____

_____

Make a list of things that start out small and grow to something bigger.

_____

_____

_____

_____

_____

List all the things around you—what tools do you have at your disposal?

_____

_____

_____

_____

_____

_____

Gratitude

Do you ever take the time to jot down what you're thankful for?

I started a gratitude journal years ago, and it transformed my life. It was a play-by-play of every tiny win happening in my world. As I'd sit down to paint or draw, I found more meaning and appreciation in what I was making. I felt more present in the process. Fueled constantly with joy, I watched as that joy overflowed into everything I created and made. When I needed inspiration for what to draw, I could pull ideas from the journal. When I needed motivation to keep going, I could look back on all the things I wrote about.

Get quiet and meditate on what gratitude means to you. Follow the prompts below, answering as you can. There's no need to rush; you can go at your own pace.

Journal about or draw a skill or talent you have that you are thankful for.

_____

_____

_____

_____

_____

_____

_____

_____

_____

Share about someone who has made an impact in your life.

_____

_____

_____

_____

_____

Share a life-changing moment or valuable lesson you've learned.

_____

_____

_____

_____

_____

Draw something you are grateful for.

Oh, give thanks
to the LORD, for
He is good! For His mercy
endures forever.

Psalm 136:1, NKJV

Daily Gratitude

Gratitude journaling is a positive step toward a more mentally healthy outlook. Follow this journal page prompt to help you start writing down what you are thankful for.

LITTLE THINGS

BIG THINGS

RELATIONSHIPS

SPIRITUAL THINGS

LIFE

WORK

Monthly Gratitude Page

Follow this journal page prompt to track what you are thankful for throughout the month.

MONTH:

Observe and Document

I get my love of documenting from my father. When I was growing up, he'd always have a camera in hand, ready to snap a photo of the family and capture memories. He had a big box full of old photos and mementos that were meaningful to him. I now find myself collecting in the same way. I love to curate boards of ideas, collect photos from my life, screenshot messages from friends, and hang on to things that mean something. This has been a crucial tool for cultivating my creativity.

Observing and documenting can serve as a launching point for creative ideas. The archive of things observed, collected, or remembered can be a treasure trove of ideas. You can look over what you've observed or gathered and allow it to help generate new ideas, innovative thoughts, and inspiration.

Give yourself space to try some of these activities to see the power of observing what is already around you:

- Pick a room, and lie down in a different area of the room than where you normally go. Look up, and point out three things you haven't noticed before that were there already.

- Pick a shape in the morning, and find all the things that are that shape while you go through your day.

- Head out on a walk, and notice all the shadows you can see.

The Power of Play

No matter if it's a made-up game or craft project, embarking in play gives us the freedom to explore and think outside the box. Play can release the pressure to be perfect and help you form unique ideas and find solutions to problems. Every day, the opportunity to play is available to you! Use the prompts below to dive into your relationship with play and discover how to tap into this valuable resource.

How did you play when you were a kid? What were your favorite games?

_____

_____

_____

_____

_____

_____

Do you believe playing is just for kids? Why?

_____

_____

_____

_____

_____

How do you have fun?

_____

_____

_____

_____

_____

Make a list of ways you like to move your body.

_____

_____

_____

_____

_____

_____

Make a list of what made you happy this week.

_____

_____

_____

_____

_____

List all the ways you engaged in play this month.

_____

_____

_____

_____

_____

_____

_____

Write a list of things you have always wanted to do.

_____

_____

_____

_____

_____

_____

_____

_____

_____

_____

You are ~~never~~
too old to
set another goal
or to dream a
new dream.

—Les Brown

Experiment with Trying New Things

It's important to our creativity to be open and try new things. Use one item from your list of things you've wanted to try from the previous activity, or come up with a new idea to use. What will you do? How will you plan for it? Record your experience by using the activity below. Feel free to use this format for each new idea you try.

Title: Date:
Inspiration:
Aim / mission:

Materials or supplies I used:

What I did:

steps

| 10% | 20% | 30% | 40% | 50% | 60% | 70% | 80% | 90% | 100% |

complete

What were the results? What happened?

Creative Challenges

Creative challenges are great for gaining consistency, trying new things, and growing in your skills. This focused attempt at creativity helps you stick to a theme and work on developing your style. Think of a medium, subject, activity, or idea that would benefit from some focused attention from you. Use the following worksheet to track your progress, consistency, and learnings.

30-Day Challenge

My challenge:

Why is this important?

Reward:

Get started

Reflections + learnings

30-Day Challenge

My challenge:

Why is this important?

Reward:

Get started

Reflections + learnings

30-Day Challenge

My challenge:

Why is this important?

Reward:

Get started

Reflections + learnings

30-Day Challenge

My challenge:

Why is this important?

Reward:

Get started

○ ○ ○ ○ ○ ○ ○ ○ ○
○ ○ ○ ○ ○ ○ ○ ○ ○
○ ○ ○ ○ ○ ○ ○ ○ ○

Reflections + learnings

you can feel

uncomfor-
table

and still show up.

-LISA CONGDON

Reflect and Celebrate

My most creative moments have often come when I am open to new ideas and new experiences in life. By using what we have, we can become more aware of possibility all around us. I hope each exercise and challenge from this section pushed you to start thinking outside the box, take risks, appreciate what you've got, and keep trying. Stay open to discovery and willing to play, and you'll be amazed at where it will lead you on your creative path.

Use the space below for your personal reflections on this section.

_____

_____

_____

_____

_____

_____

_____

_____

Celebrate today

by going for a short walk in your neighborhood or local park. Observe your surroundings, let go of your worries, and connect with nature as a way to celebrate how far you've come.

_____

_____

_____

_____

_____

Be Encouraged

There are so many incredible artists out there. If you ever need to be inspired by fellow creatives, take time to read through these quotes.

The world may be a crowded place, but there is still room for you, room for you to tell your story and to create things and contribute things that make a difference.

—MORGAN HARPER NICHOLS

If we want to create inspiring art, we have to consume inspiring art. We have to go where the light is, toward what is lovely, toward what makes us feel alive.

—ASHLEE GADD

Connecting & Sharing Your Message

Our Creator made each thing in our world with intention. That's the same way we get to approach our gifts and what we choose to make with them.

Maybe you're doing what you are with your art simply because you can and you want to honor God. That's honestly one of the best reasons. But God may also have more planned, and it's important to have an open heart for those possibilities.

As I practiced and shared the gifts God gave me, I began to understand that my artistic voice was important and needed to be heard. There weren't a lot of people like me, a Black woman, in the field. I was lonely and terrified to step out into this unknown space. But the more I focused on creating as worship, the stronger the message of my work grew.

Why do you create? What message, feeling, or encouragement do you see unfolding as you use and share your gifts? This section will help you answer these questions and find meaning in what you do, appreciate your journey, and be encouraged in shining your light, as well as plan out how you want to do it. Let's get started!

Connect to Your HeArt

Looking back at the roads you have traveled can give you hints about the things that are important to you and why you create what you do. The questions below aim to help you discover how what you create connects to your heart and how you get to use it to connect and share your *heArt* with those around you.

What lights you up? What makes you excited?

_____

_____

_____

List everything you feel passionate about. What are your hopes, your God-given gifts, and things you are on fire for?

_____

_____

_____

_____

How have your past experiences helped you become who you are today?

_____

_____

_____

_____

List any specific messages that keep coming to mind as you make, write, paint, etc.

_____

_____

_____

_____

_____

List any themes you see consistently in what you share, talk about, or create.

_____

_____

_____

_____

_____

_____

What issues, people, or things do you care deeply for?

_____

_____

_____

_____

_____

How do you naturally give and show up for others in need?

_____

_____

_____

_____

_____

What do friends always seem to ask you for help with or advice about?
How can you use your creativity toward that area?

_____

_____

_____

_____

_____

What words would you use to describe the things you have created?
Ask a friend.

_____

_____

_____

_____

_____

What is something that's hard to get you to stop talking about once you start?

_____

_____

_____

_____

_____

List the greatest compliments and encouragement you've received.

_____

_____

_____

_____

_____

Write out the ways that where you are right now fulfills the dreams and desires of your past.

_____

_____

_____

_____

_____

Find Inspiration in Your Past Work

Each year, I make it a point to review what I've created in the past. Although I often have self-critiques, I can usually see themes, recurring ideas, or messages portrayed in what I've created. Reflecting can bring much-needed perspective and appreciation for how far you've come. It also works as a tool to help inspire you for the future.

List some of the most meaningful things that you have done or created. Dedicate a few minutes to work through the sections below to evaluate each of your creations.

Portfolio Tracker

CREATIVE PROJECT: _____

Description: _____

_____

_____

Tools and materials: _____

_____

What was the process? _____

_____

What impact does it have on me? _____

_____

What did I learn? _____

_____

_____

CREATIVE PROJECT:

_____

Description: _____

_____

_____

Tools and materials: _____

_____

What was the process? _____

_____

What impact does it have on me? _____

_____

What did I learn? _____

_____

_____

CREATIVE PROJECT:

_____

Description: _____

_____

_____

Tools and materials: _____

_____

What was the process? _____

_____

What impact does it have on me? _____

_____

What did I learn? _____

_____

_____

Revisiting Your Creative Why

Review your responses from the last few pages. Does anything stand out? What recurring themes do you spot as you reflect on these questions? What have you been expressing and saying in your work?

Next, use this worksheet and revisit your creative why from when you began this journal (page 52). What changes do you feel need to be made?

Develop an updated why statement. As you continue to ask yourself why to each response you give below, you will get closer to understanding what is driving you forward. Remember, as you grow, you can always come back and revisit it.

I create because . . .

Why?

Why?

Why?

Why?

I create because . . .

Share Your Light

You are valuable, and each part of you was carefully placed within you. God values your creative gifts and gave them to you with intention. He wants you to use your gifts and not hide them. When you share your gifts, you create and connect to the world around you, love and encourage others, and remind yourself that God's love lives in you.

Art in any form can often speak louder than words. It can even help with healing in times of difficulty or devastation. Creating in tough times is not always easy, but it's an opportunity to share light with the world around you. You never know just how much your light might matter to someone else's life.

Give yourself a moment to reflect on the prompts that follow. Feel free to complete them at your own pace.

Share about a time when something you created benefited someone else.

Sometimes the **HARDEST** part of the journey is believing **YOU ARE** worth the trip.

— GLENN BECK

Write out simple ways you've enjoyed being kind to others.

Share about a time when something someone did for you impacted your life dramatically.

List the gifts you want to give to others through what you do, what you say or write, and what you make.

List the opportunities (things, people, and experiences) you want to say yes to.

What do you hope others say, feel, or experience when they are around you? How can you show this in your creative work?

Write out the feelings you'd want someone to experience when interacting with your creation.

Create with Purpose

Now that you've worked through discovering more of your message, what can you intentionally create going forward?

Jot down some ideas or new perspectives you've gained from working through this section. What can you try with purpose in mind?

- _____
- _____
- _____
- _____
- _____
- _____
- _____
- _____
- _____
- _____
- _____
- _____

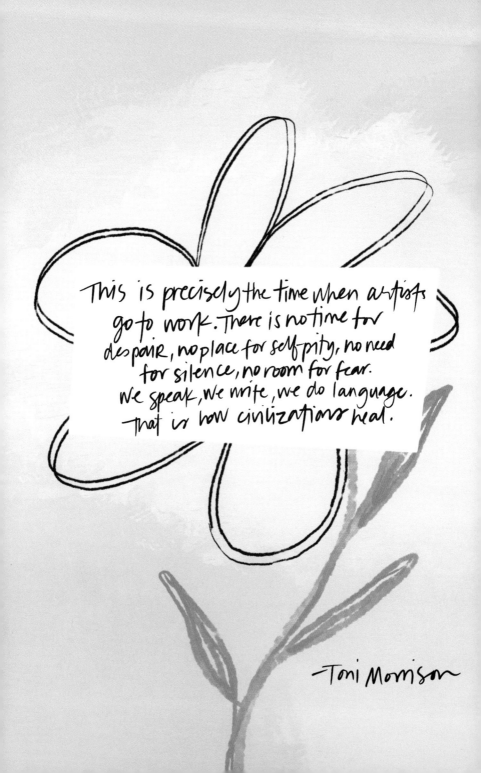

This is precisely the time when artists go to work. There is no time for despair, no place for self pity, no need for silence, no room for fear. We speak, we write, we do language. That is how civilizations heal.

—Toni Morrison

Plan to Share

You're now to the point where it's time to plan how you will showcase and share your gift!

Think about where you're going to do this. Maybe you want to share your poem with friends at your next get-together or gift what you've made to a family member. Perhaps you are hoping to showcase your art in a local gallery or are going to put it on your blog or social media. However you choose to share your art, it's important to make a plan and follow through!

Take a moment to jot down ideas for where you can share your next creative work.

_____

_____

_____

_____

_____

Next, make a list of the steps you'll need to take to get it completed.

_____

_____

_____

_____

_____

Use the calendar below to plan out when you will do each action step.
Color each circle the color you worked on each day.

Monthly Creative Goals

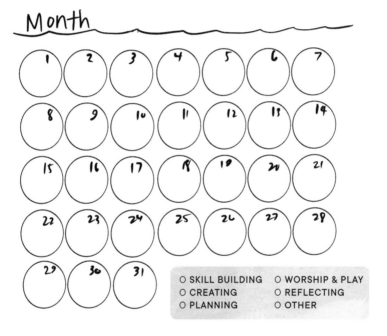

Month _____

1	2	3	4	5	6	7
8	9	10	11	12	13	14
15	16	17	18	19	20	21
22	23	24	25	26	27	28
29	30	31				

O SKILL BUILDING   O WORSHIP & PLAY
O CREATING   O REFLECTING
O PLANNING   O OTHER

Materials I'm using:

Notes & reflections: _____

Reflect and Celebrate

When we are present and connected to ourselves and what we create, we start to see how much of an impact the things that flow from us have. Our passion and heart help fuel us to make and share effective, influential creations. Allow yourself time to reflect on the guidance in this section, the messages you've uncovered within your work, and the why that has been evident in the past and continues to propel you forward. How might you continue to show up and share?

Use the space below for your personal reflections on this section.

_____

_____

_____

_____

_____

_____

_____

_____

_____

_____

_____

_____

Time for one more celebration!

Text or call a friend, and share with them what you are most proud of from working through this book.

Be Encouraged

There are so many incredible artists out there. If you ever need to be inspired by fellow creatives, take time to read through these quotes.

A lot of people don't understand that some creative human being is on the beginning end of everything that's essential to our civilised world.

—LUBAINA HIMID

It is unimportant (and perhaps impossible) to be totally original. But YOU are an original and I am an original, so the best way to produce creative work is to inject as much of yourself, your personal style, your experiences into it as possible.

—JUSTINA BLAKENEY

Take time
to let go
and be.

Your Journey Continues

Romans 12:6 beautifully says, "Having gifts . . . let us use them."

I've shared my personal way through the creative process and tools that help me dive deeper into my gifts. But how things flow for me might not work for you. So, now it's your turn to find your creative practice and process. Take what you've learned, and use your gifts.

If you're feeling stuck or aren't sure how to move through the process, then you can turn back to the creative map. Use it, along with the exercises throughout the book, as your starting point. The following pages offer you a few extra brain dumps to help you continue your journey. In whatever way you choose to work through your journey, spend time with God and use your gifts; be encouraged, because the potential is truly in your hands.

Having gifts that differ according to the
grace given to us, let us use them: if prophecy,
in proportion to our faith; if service, in
our serving; the one who teaches, in his teaching;
the one who exhorts, in his exhortation; the one who
contributes, in generosity; the one who leads,
with zeal; the one who does acts of
mercy, with cheerfulness.
(Romans 12:6–8)

Brain Dump

Brain Dump

Brain Dump

Bibliography

Balfour, Danielle Coke. *A Heart on Fire: 100 Meditations on Loving Your Neighbors Well*. Kansas City, Mo.: Andrews McMeel, 2023.

Blakeney, Justina. "On Creativity." Justina's Journal (blog). July 25, 2016. https://blog.justinablakeney.com/2016/07/on-creativity.html.

Bonney, Grace. *In the Company of Women: Inspiration and Advice from over 100 Makers, Artists, and Entrepreneurs*. New York: Artisan, 2016.

Brown, Clint, comp. *Artist to Artist: Inspiration and Advice from Artists Past and Present*. Corvallis, Ore.: Jackson Creek, 1998.

"Creative Types." Adobe Create. https://mycreativetype.com/the-creative-types.

"Creativity with Ruth Chou Simons." *Journeywomen*. Podcast. November 13, 2017. https://journeywomenpodcast.com/episode/2017/7/ep27-on-creativity.

Gadd, Ashlee. *Create Anyway: The Joy of Pursuing Creativity in the Margins of Motherhood*. Minneapolis: Bethany House, 2023.

Himid, Lubaina. "'After Lockdown, There Are Decisions to Be Made. Are the Arts Essential, or a Nice Luxury?'" Royal Academy. May 20, 2020. www.royalacademy.org.uk/article/artists-in-isolation-lubaina-himid.

Jokic, Natasha. "There Are 4 Types of Creative People in the World: Which One Are You?" BuzzFeed. June 10, 2020. www.buzzfeed.com/natashajokic1/creative-type-quiz.

Nichols, Morgan Harper. *Storyteller: 100 Poem Letters*. Self-published, CreateSpace, 2017.

Tchaikovsky, Modeste. *The Life and Letters of Peter Ilich Tchaikovsky*. Vol. 1, edited by Rosa Newmarch. New York: Vienna House, 1973.

Vonnegut, Kurt. *If This Isn't Nice, What Is?: Advice for the Young*. Compiled by Dan Wakefield. New York: Seven Stories Press, 2014.

Wagner, Meta. *What's Your Creative Type?: Harness the Power of Your Artistic Personality*. Berkeley, Calif.: Seal Press, 2017.

About the Author

JENA HOLLIDAY is a full-time artist, writer, entrepreneur, and storyteller from Minnesota. She is the creator and owner of Spoonful of Faith illustration and design studio, as well as the author of *Sacred Creativity* and the children's book *A Spoonful of Faith*.

   With just a bit of faith, she walked away from her mainstream marketing job to embrace her passion for art. What started as a hobby eventually evolved into a full-time commitment of spreading kindness and hope through her artwork and words. That commitment blossomed into a blog and shop, aptly named Spoonful of Faith, and has become not only a successful business but also a cultural beacon.

   Holliday wants her journey and her illustrations to motivate others, especially women, to face fear, find their voices, and walk boldly in all God has for them.

spoonfuloffaith.com
Instagram: @aspoonfuloffaith / @spoonfuloffaithstudio